The Guide to Dating for Teenagers with Asperger Syndrome

The Guide to Dating for Teenagers with Asperger Syndrome

Jeannie Uhlenkamp

Foreword by Diane Adreon

© 2009 Autism Asperger Publishing Co.
P.O. Box 23173
Shawnee Mission, Kansas 66283-0173
www.asperger.net

Publisher's Cataloging-in-Publication

Uhlenkamp, Jeannie.

The guide to dating for teenagers with Asperger syndrome / Jeannie Uhlenkamp. -- 1st ed. -- Shawnee Mission, Kan. : Autism Asperger Pub. Co., c2009.

p. ; cm.
ISBN: 978-1-934575-53-6
LCCN: 2009929574
Includes bibliographical references.

1. Asperger's syndrome in adolescence--Patients--Social aspects. 2. Dating (Social customs) 3. Teenagers--Conduct of life. 4. Social skills in adolescence. 5. Adolescent psychology. I. Title.

RJ506.A9 U45 2009
618.92/858832--dc22   0907

Illustration on front cover ©shutterstock.com.

This book is designed in Helvetica Neue and American Typewriter.

Printed in the United States of America.

Dedication

This book is dedicated to my husband, Mike,

who has been incredibly supportive,

Sarah H., and to all my friends at N.E. Metro 916.

J.U.

Foreword

Youngsters with AS are often "immature" for their chronological age. Therefore, it makes sense for parents and professionals to assume that it will take our kids longer to adopt various aspects of young adult life. Even so, this does not mean that we should wait to teach them about dating. In all likelihood, given their prevailing core characteristics, our kids will need more time and more practice to learn strategies for navigating the complexities of male-female friendships and relationships. After all, this is a challenging area for a high percentage of neurotypicals as well.

Although dating guides have been written for the general public, until now very little has been written specifically for individuals with Asperger Syndrome on this topic. Fortunately, Jeannie Uhlenkamp has come to our rescue by writing a book addressing some of the male-female social relationship challenges adolescents with Asperger Syndrome are likely to encounter.

This dating guide for teenagers with Asperger Syndrome is WONDERFUL. It is written in a Dear Abby format and covers getting acquainted and dating, the inevitable break-up that teens are likely to experience, as well as everything else in between. Each question and answer includes a set of discussion questions and a summary of the main idea. In addition, definitions of words the teenager with AS may not understand (e.g., infatuation, nerve-wracking) are included.

This book will serve as a valuable resource for teens with AS, as well as their parents and teachers. Clinicians will also be thrilled to discover this user-friendly resource. *The Guide to Dating for Teenagers with Asperger Syndrome* can be used as a "dating curriculum" for a group of teens, in individual therapy, or by a parent talking through these issues with his/her teen.

> – Diane Adreon, associate director, UM-NSU Center for Autism & Related Disabilities, University of Miami; co-author (with Brenda Myles) of *Asperger Syndrome and Adolescence: Practical Solutions for School Success*, winner of the Autism Society of America's Outstanding Literary Work of the Year

Dear Reader,

Welcome to *The Guide to Dating for Teenagers with Asperger Syndrome*. It is my hope that teens and adults will use entries in this book to discuss the complexities of dating. This guide is meant to be used either at home with parents or friends, or at school as part of a supplementary social skills curriculum.

First, I'd like you to know that I am not a counselor, but rather a special education teacher. Because initiating, maintaining, and ending a dating relationship can be so intense and so potentially confusing, many students I work with have questions about the social complexities of dating. This book was written in response to those questions. While the information will not tell teens exactly "how to" date, my hope is that it will generate many useful discussions about what dating is like.

When I started researching this intriguing topic, I found that there weren't many resources specifically designed to guide teens with Asperger Syndrome through the dating process. The best resources I have found include some Internet sites such as about.com and books such as *The Complete Idiot's Guide to Dating for Teens* by Susan Rabens and *The How Rude Handbook of Friendship and Dating Manners for Teens: Surviving the Social Scene* by Alex J. Packer. Though these books do not directly address Asperger Syndrome, the information given is very relevant to anyone struggling to understand the social implications of dating. There are also additional resources at the back of this book.

I decided to follow a format of questions and answers for this text – much like you would find in a newspaper advice column – in order to address realistic questions in an easy-to-follow format. Fictional teens have "written in" to ask questions of teens Jerome and Haley, who do their best to answer dating questions and offer advice on how to navigate the dating world. Also, for each entry, there are Discussion Questions to further explore and personalize issues. If you are a young person reading this, remember that even if a question is asked by a young man, it is probably still very relevant to a young woman, or vice versa.

While this guide doesn't offer all the answers to common dating issues, it offers many insights and practical suggestions. It is divided into sections on topics ranging from the first date to the last kiss, and it addresses many situations in between as well as a "just wondering" section. At the end of each entry, you will also find a "Main Idea" section, which sums up one general rule of dating related to the question being raised. In addition, throughout the book there are *Notes* explaining either language or social nuances (presented in boldface print) that may be confusing to a person on the autism spectrum.

If you decide to date, make sure you have someone in your life you can talk to directly about your dating questions. In this book, I refer to that person as a "trusted adult" and that means any adult with whom you feel comfortable discussing matters of this nature (such as a parent, family member, or counselor). These adults can be invaluable to you, especially when things seem confusing or when you are confronted by serious situations, so be sure to seek them out for advice and assistance.

To teenagers reading this, I would like to say a sincere, "Best wishes!" Dating can be fun and exciting; it also can have moments of heartbreak, embarrassment, and disappointment. Everyone who dates feels this at one point or another, especially in the beginning. You are not alone! **Just try to learn something from every person and every date you have, because it's all part of the dating experience**.

Good luck in all your dating adventures!

Sincerely,

Jeannie Uhlenkamp

Table of Contents

Part One: Getting to Know You 1

  How Do I Know if She "Likes" Me?........................... 2

  Asking Him Out.. 4

  Sweating a Lot... 6

  How Do I Accept a Date? 8

  With My Sensory Issues, Can I Really Date? 10

  Does He Just Want a Physical Relationship? 12

  What Should I Talk About? 14

  What Does Having Asperger Syndrome Mean

      for Me and Dating?....................................... 16

  She Gives Me an Excuse When I Call..................... 18

  Interested, But too Nervous to Ask Him Out.............. 20

  How Can I Start the Conversation?........................ 22

  My First Date Was a Disaster! 24

  Should I Call Her?... 26

  Asking Her Out 28

  Is It O.K. to Date Someone I Met Online?................. 30

Part Two: Officially Dating.. 33

  Are My Expectations Getting in the Way? 34

  My Boyfriend Likes to Party 36

  I'm Meeting the Parents!.................................... 38

  Some Things About My Date Annoy Me 40

  How Can I Make It up to Her? 42

  Special Song... 44

  Getting Possessive 46

  A Birthday Present 48

  Someone Wants Me to Break up With My Boyfriend .. 50

  Impressing My Date 52

  He Keeps Interrupting Me................................... 54

  Wanting to Slow It Down 56

  Standing up for Me too Much 58

  Nosey Friend... 60

  Is Dating Competitive?...................................... 62

Bothered by His Friend 64

Wishing for Perfection.. 66

Only Doing What He Wants to Do 68

Table Manners 70

Still Upset After an Argument.................................. 72

How Can I Tell if Things Are Getting Serious?............. 74

Dating Two People at the Same Time.................... 76

Is It Over? 78

Another Girl Called Me, and My Girlfriend Got Mad 80

Picking a Fight 82

Anger Issues 84

Deciding Whether or Not to Have Sex.................... 86

May I Kiss You? 88

Part Three: When It's Over............................... 91

Is It O.K. to Break up Over the Phone?.................. 92

How Do I Tell Him to Give Me My Space? 94

Can I Date My Friend's Ex? 96

Can We Still Be Friends? 98

I Still "Like" My Ex 100

We Broke up, and I Feel Lousy 102

Part Four: Just Wondering 105

Is It Weird NOT to Date? 106

Attractiveness.. 108

Am I Gay?.. 110

How Can I Learn More About Dating?.................. 112

Is It O.K. to Be in Love With My Teacher? 114

Will I Ever Go on a Date? 116

Masturbation.. 118

Are There Things You Just Don't Say? 120

What Are They Talking About? 122

Resources 125

Part One:

Getting to Know You

How Do I Know If She "Likes" Me?

Dear Jerome,

I am a 15-year-old boy. I like a girl in my school named Jessica. How do I know if she **likes me back**?

Jack

Dear Jack,

Ah yes, this is one of the most difficult questions of all when it comes to dating. Just how *do* you know that someone likes you in the way that you like him or her? While I don't claim to know everything there is to know about dating, here are some starters.

A girl may like you if she goes out of her way to talk to you. She may like you if she stands close to you or offers to sit by you. She may like you if she gives you compliments like, "You're so funny!" or "You're so smart." She may like you if she gives you invitations to spend time with her like, "We should hang out some time."

My advice to you is this: Take it slow. If she keeps talking to you, goes out of her way to see you, and gives you positive attention, she may like you the way you like her, and you may be ready for the next step.

Of course, there is the possibility that this girl is just a nice person or is simply being nice to you without wishing to date you. You could try asking a friend to help you find out if she likes you as more than just a friend. The best situation would be if you are friends with one of her friends; you could ask that person to ask her for you.

Best wishes!

Jerome

Discussion Questions

- How can you tell if someone really "likes" you?

- What are you afraid of when it comes to "liking" someone?

- Did you ever think someone liked you, but he or she really didn't? What happened?

- Why is it sometimes hard to tell if someone "likes" you?

- What are some good ways to ask friends to find out if another person "likes" you?

Main Idea: A good way to find out if someone "likes" you is to ask a mutual friend to find out for you.

Note: "Likes you" in this case means the other person is interested in dating you, or is interested in you in a romantic way. This is the same as "likes you more than just a friend."

Asking Him Out

Dear Haley,

I am a 16-year-old girl. I like this guy in my class who is friends with my friend, Annie, and I want to ask him out. I don't know him that well, and I don't even know what he likes to do. Should I just ask him out?

Becca

Dear Becca,

So you want to ask this boy out but are unsure of what he will say? This is called the "unknown," and there's not a person alive who hasn't felt afraid of this one! The good news is that the situation may turn out great, but it may help to do a little **detective work** before doing the asking.

Here's something you could try. Since Annie is already friends with this guy, why don't you ask her to help you out? She could help you by telling you what he likes to do – movies, games, sports, or whatever. If she knows the guy, she probably knows some of these things. You could also ask Annie to find out, subtly, if the boy would go out with you or not. *Subtly* means that maybe Annie could say something to him like, "You know Becca, right? She's really cool. She's also a friend of mine, and I was wondering if the two of you would like to do something with my boyfriend and me this weekend."

Best wishes!

Haley

Discussion Questions

- Have you ever been afraid to ask someone out on a date?

- Have you ever asked a friend to help you get to know someone you're interested in dating?

- Have you ever been rejected when someone didn't want to go out with you? If so, what happened?

- Has there ever been anyone you really wanted to date but never asked out?

Main Idea: You can always ask a friend to help you get to know someone you'd like to date.

Note: "Detective work" in this case means trying to find out information without being obvious that you're trying to find out information.

Sweating a Lot

Dear Jerome,

I would really like to ask out this one really cute girl, but every time I see her, I get nervous and my armpits start sweating really, really bad. What's worse is that when this happens, my body odor gets really bad, too. I am afraid that all this will drive her away. What should I do?

Antwon

Dear Antwon,

Man! That's tough! When I was a teenager I had the same problem. Whenever I'd get nervous – like for a test at school or asking a girl out – my arm pits would overflow like a raging river! It seemed that even when I used a deodorant and showered frequently, nothing would help!

Then one day our health instructor at school gave me some really good advice. He said that I shouldn't apply antiperspirant/deodorant right after I took a shower, but to wait until later when my armpits were totally dry. Also, he said that sometimes it's helpful to try different types of antiperspirants/ deodorants to find the one that works for your specific body. Try one at a time, and when you find a product that works for you, you may want to apply it several times a day at school (like in the bathroom or the nurse's office), especially after playing sports.

If nothing you find works, talk to your family and decide if you want to ask a doctor for advice.

One other strategy you may wish to try involves keeping yourself from feeling that nervous to begin with. You could try to identify what makes you really nervous and then make a plan for how to deal with it. For example, it may make you nervous to talk one-to-one with a girl. In that case, you may need to take few deep breaths before approaching her and tell yourself it will be O.K., or you may wish to see her in another setting such as when she's with a group of friends.

It may help to know that perspiration problems are very common among teenagers whose bodies and hormones are changing rapidly. Hopefully, something will work for you, and you won't have to deal with this any longer!

Best wishes!

Jerome

Discussion Questions

- Have you ever had problems with sweating? If so, what happened?

- What helps you to relax when you're nervous?

- What do you use to control sweat?

- Why do we sweat anyway?

Main Idea: Try to plan strategies in advance of events that make you nervous, and if you still sweat a lot, find a reliable deodorant.

How Do I Accept a Date?

Dear Haley,

There's a guy I know in school, and I've heard he is going to ask me out on a date. If he does, what should I say?

Dianna

Dear Dianna,

There are many ways to accept or reject an offer of a date. The main question to answer is, Do you want to go out with this guy? If your answer is yes, you can simply say something like, "Sure. That sounds great!" or "Yeah, I'm free then. That would work." Then you'd want to make sure you also knew all the details of when and where you'll meet, or whether or not he needs directions to your house.

If you don't want to go out with him, it gets a little tricky in that if you just flat out say "no," you may end up hurting his feelings. Commonly, when a person doesn't want to date someone, they either say that they are busy and can't, or they make up some other excuse why they can't go out. If you really are busy, however, be sure to tell him that it's not just an excuse and then offer a different date and time that would work for you.

Another thing to consider saying if you don't want to go out with someone is, "I'd like to just be friends with you and not date." This is a common thing to do as well.

Best wishes!

Haley

 # Discussion Questions

- What are some good ways you can accept a date?

- What are some good ways you can decline dating someone?

- Would you feel comfortable making up an excuse to decline a date?

- What would you do if a person kept asking you out and you were not interested in dating them?

 **Main Idea: Saying "no" to someone who asks you out can be difficult. When you do want to say "no," it is common to make up an excuse as to why you can't meet with the person, or to simply say that you prefer to stay friends and not date.**

With My Sensory Issues, Can I Really Date?

Dear Jerome,

I have a lot of opportunities to ask girls on dates, but I don't really want to because of my sensory issues. For example, I can't take a lot of light, noise, smells, or touch. I feel like a sensory nightmare! Any advice?

Marcus

Dear Marcus,

I guess the first question I would ask myself would be, "Do I want to date?" If the answer to that is "yes," then you may need to tell your date about your sensory needs and make plans for how you can **accommodate** for them.

For example, if you don't like noise or lights, you may want avoid places like malls and choose more low-key activities, like going for a hike or to a coffee shop. Just be sure to talk to your date about what you like to do and dislike to do, and why. Ideally, your date would also like quiet things, but if she doesn't, you may need to take that into consideration and do the things she likes to do sometimes as well. In these cases, it may be helpful to give yourself "sensory breaks." For example, if you go to the mall, don't plan to stay all day. Stay for shorter amounts of time and head outside every once in a while for a break.

Sensory issues of touch are trickier, as physical touch can be a sign of intimacy. If you have sensory issues, again, know what you like and what you don't like, and try to explain your preferences to your date. For example, if you don't like to hug and she does, let her know that it's nothing personal. Explain that you don't like the way it feels and suggest you do something else, such as sitting close to one another or holding hands for a while.

Best wishes!

Jerome

Discussion Questions

- What sorts of sensory issues bother you? (Consider: touch, taste, sounds, sights, smells.)

- What do you do to adjust to sensory needs?

- How can you tell someone, politely, that you don't like some things such as hugs?

- Can you "make" yourself get used to sensory over-load?

Main Idea: If you do have sensory issues, be sure you know what your needs are, explain them to your date, and make accommodations for them.

Note: "Accommodate" means making changes to suit your needs. For example, if you dislike loud music and are going to an indoor concert, consider wearing ear plugs for part of the performance, or plan to take a break by going outside.

Does He Just Want a Physical Relationship?

Dear Haley,

I have heard that some guys want to date a girl just to have sex with her. Is that true?

Tabitha

Dear Tabitha,

First off, yes, it is true that some guys are only interested in physical relationships with girls, and when they get that, they break up with them. It is also true that some guys may say, "I love you" or make promises that aren't true just to have sex. These are the kind of guys to watch out for.

There is good news, however. Not all guys are like that. If you respect yourself and say "no" to physical contact that you don't want, most guys will respect you and your wishes.

If you do find yourself feeling pressure to have sex – or any kind of physical intimacy that you feel you are not ready for – it may be time to break up with the guy and date someone else who respects you and your wishes. And, if you are in a situation in which you are feeling pressure to have sex and are unsure of what to do, be sure to talk to a trusted adult!

Best wishes!

Haley

 # Discussion Questions

- Have you heard of guys who only want **one thing** from their dates?

- Why might a disrespectful date break up with someone who won't have a physical relationship with him?

- Have you ever thought about what kind of relationship you are ready for physically?

- What would your ideal relationship be like at this time?

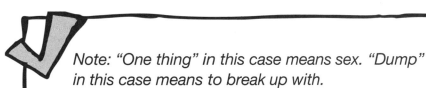

Main Idea: Some guys only want to have sex with their dates. If their dates won't have sex with them, they *dump* them for someone who will.

Note: "One thing" in this case means sex. "Dump" in this case means to break up with.

What Should I Talk About?

Dear Jerome,

I'm planning on taking this one girl out on a date. I'm really nervous, though, because I like her, but I have no idea what to talk to her about. What should I say?

Rick

Dear Rick,

Having a conversation with your date can be both interesting and also difficult. I think everyone struggles at times with what to say, especially when the room gets quiet. Try to think of talking with your date as a way to get to know her. Think especially about what *she may like to talk about* and about what *interests her*. In general, people like to talk a lot about these two topics. For example, you may know that your date is interested in movies. Read up on some current movies, and then ask her questions such as: "What kind of movies do you like?" "Do you have a favorite movie?" "Do you think there are any good movies playing right now?"

When you hear her answers, you may wish to take your date to a movie and then discuss the movie afterwards. Ironically, the key to being a good conversationalist is not necessarily what you say, but *how well you listen*.

Another conversation tip is to talk about things you both have in common. For example, if you are in the same classes or extracurricular activities, you could talk about those.

Finally, always remember to be yourself and don't try too hard. Part of dating is acceptance; both accepting yourself and the other person. And sometimes it's just nice to be with the other person, whether you're talking or not!

Best wishes!

Jerome

 # Discussion Questions

- What do teenagers usually enjoy talking about?

- How do you show a person that you're really listening?

- What should you do if you are not interested in the topic of conversation, but it's a subject that the other person likes to talk about?

Main Idea: The key to having a good conversation with someone is to ask questions about things that interest them and then focus on topics that interest you both.

What Does Having Asperger Syndrome Mean for Me and Dating?

Dear Haley,

I recently found out that I have Asperger Syndrome. What might this mean for dating? Am I ever going to go out on a date?

Kelly

Dear Kelly,

So you have Asperger Syndrome – that's a good thing to know. It's always good to know as much about ourselves as possible, both the easy parts of our personalities and the challenges. I presume your teachers, parents, and others have talked to you about Asperger Syndrome, and perhaps you've looked up information about it and have some idea about what it means for you. If you don't know much about Asperger Syndrome, I encourage you to do research and find out as much as you can about what it is and how it may affect you – both positively and negatively. Check out the resource list in the back of this book. Also, your parents and teachers may be good sources of information and offer valuable insights.

Having Asperger Syndrome may mean that you have certain intense interests. It may also mean that it is difficult for you to understand what your date may be thinking or feeling because reading body language or picking up visual cues is a challenge for you. If this is the case, you may need to practice the skills of reading others' body language, especially their facial expressions. There are many books and computer programs that can help you with this. You may also need to practice skills in having conversations. For example, practice taking your turn in a conversation on any given topic – even if it's a topic you don't care for.

Dating is difficult for lots of people, and many people share, to one degree or another, the same traits you may have. My advice to you is to relax. We all wonder about dating and tend to have very high expectations of the experience. The best is when you can find someone you like and who makes you feel good when you're around him. When you find that someone, you will know.

Best wishes,

Haley

Discussion Questions

- What are the general characteristics of Asperger Syndrome?

- What are your strengths and challenges?

- Why is it good for all of us to "know ourselves"?

- What do you really enjoy doing with other people?

- What can you gain by listening to someone talk about his or her interests?

Main Idea: Anyone can date, and dating in its most basic form means spending time with someone you enjoy being with.

She Gives Me an Excuse When I Call

Dear Jerome,

I've asked a girl on a date several times now, and she always seems to have an excuse for why she can't go out with me. Should I stop asking?

Warren

Dear Warren,

In general, if you ask a girl out on a date and she comes up with an excuse more than once, she probably is not that interested in going out with you.

Of course, there are times when she really may be busy, or she has already made plans. In such cases, if she really wanted to go out with you, she would say something like, "I'm sorry, but I've already got some plans with my parents on Friday night. I'm free Saturday though!"

But if she says something like, "I'm washing my hair that night" or, "I don't want to miss my favorite TV show," give up right there, because these are all code words for one very small word, "no."

Best wishes!

Jerome

 # Discussion Questions

- Why would someone make up an excuse not to go out with another person? Why wouldn't they just tell the other person that they aren't interested?

- What are some excuses people use when they don't want to go out on a date?

- Have you ever made up an excuse so that you would not have to spend time with someone? If so, what was it, and how did it work out?

Main Idea: If a person is making up excuses not to see you, she doesn't wish to see you, and you should stop calling her.

Interested, But too Nervous to Ask Him Out

Dear Haley,

I am interested in dating this guy I think is really good-looking. The problem is, I'm afraid to ask him out. Whenever I see him, I get all nervous and feel embarrassed. When this happens, I can't seem to say anything at all. What should I do?

Patty

Dear Patty,

It sounds like you are really interested in this guy. First, it may help you to know that your reaction is perfectly normal. Perhaps you are even infatuated with this guy. When you are infatuated with someone, you may get very nervous around that person and perhaps sweat, blush, giggle, or even forget what you're going to say. These are all bodily reactions to strong emotions, and they're normal, especially for teenagers.

To help you overcome your nervousness, I suggest first trying to spend time with the guy in a group and to find out if there are things about him you like other than the fact that he is attractive. I think you'll find that the more time you spend together, the less your body will react in such a dramatic way, and you'll start to feel more comfortable. Ask your friends to help you and suggest a **group date**, or show up where he's likely to be. For example, if he's on the basketball team, go to some of his games.

Best wishes!

Haley

 # Discussion Questions

- Have you ever been infatuated with someone? If so, what did it feel like?

- Have you ever gotten completely **flustered** when trying to talk with someone you were interested in?

- Why might someone feel nervous around someone she is infatuated with?

- How does infatuation fade away?

 **Main Idea: Infatuation is the first stage of love. It is a temporary, intense feeling of being overwhelmed and in awe of someone you are attracted to, and it is perfectly normal to feel nervous during this stage of a relationship. To ease your discomfort, try coming into contact with that person in a group setting.**

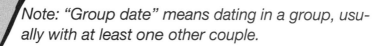 Note: "Group date" means dating in a group, usually with at least one other couple.

"Flustered" means really nervous. When you are flustered, you may do such things as become forgetful or clumsy.

How Can I Start the Conversation?

Dear Jerome,

I was at a party a couple of weeks ago, and I saw a beautiful girl across the room. I wanted to talk to her but couldn't think of one thing to say, so I didn't even go near her. If I see her again, or if this happens with somebody else, what should I say?

Brian

Dear Brian,

What you were suffering from at the party is something I like to call, "The Opening Line Problem." Many guys have become **tongue-tied** in these types of situations. You see an attractive girl across the room, you get the courage to approach her, and then ... well, then what?

Some classic "opening lines" that you may already have heard include: "Do you come here often?" and "What's a nice girl like you doing at a place like this?" My advice to you is: Do *not* use those lines! They are old-fashioned. In fact, these lines are typically used as examples of unsuccessful attempts to approach someone.

Instead, try approaching the girl with confidence – smile, and then either make a simple statement like: "Nice party, huh?" or ask a question such as, "Do you know many people here?" Then go from there depending on her response.

Most girls would be flattered that you noticed them and made the effort to come over and talk.

Better luck next time!

Jerome

Discussion Questions

- Have you ever wanted to talk to someone in a social situation but didn't know what to say? What happened?

- What's a good way to start a conversation at a party?

- Even if you start the conversation out right, could a person still choose not to talk to you?

Main Idea: When you want to talk to someone, have a few things in mind about what you could say or ask, and choose the best option. Oh, and don't forget to smile – that goes a long way!

Note: "Tongue-tied" means not being able to think of anything to say, so you don't talk at all.

My First Date Was a Disaster!

Dear Haley,

The first ever date of my life turned out to be a complete disaster. I kept saying stupid things, and then for a long time during the date, we hardly talked to each other or even looked at each other. Is there any hope for me to date again?

Mickey

Dear Mickey,

I'm sorry to hear that your date didn't turn out so well. Believe it or not though, this sort of thing happens all the time to people who date. Sometimes things just don't go that smoothly, and you find out that you aren't all that interested in each other after all. This doesn't mean that you can't date again, and, in fact, having a few dates that **bomb** is only natural.

What you might want to consider doing is to analyze the date from the perspective of: What went well? What could have gone better? What might you do differently next time?

Whatever you do, don't give up! Dating has its ups and downs, and we all have a few stories of dates we'd like to forget because they didn't go well.

Best wishes!

Haley

# Discussion Questions

- Have you ever had a date go poorly?

- Why do some dates end up being not very fun?

- Do you have a tendency to **beat yourself up** if things don't go right for you, or can you forgive yourself easily?

- What can you learn from having a bad time on a date?

Main Idea: Most people go on at least some dates that end up being not very fun, and even a bit awkward. It's a natural part of dating.

Notes: "Bomb" in this case means "doesn't go well." "Beat yourself up" in this case means "to feel badly about yourself and tell yourself negative comments."

Should I Call Her?

Dear Jerome,

I went out on a date with a girl a couple of days ago, and I'm not sure if she wants to go out with me again or not. She said I could call her again some time, but I don't want to call her now because I'm afraid she doesn't really want to go out with me. What should I do?

Chuck

Dear Chuck,

Probably when you asked this girl out on the first date you didn't know if she would go out with you until you asked. Well, if you don't ask, you'll never know if a girl will go out with you for the first date, the second date, or any date for that matter. Though this may be difficult to do because you're nervous, my advice is to give the girl a call and talk to her. If the conversation goes well, consider asking her out again. However, if she sounds like she is no longer interested and doesn't want to commit to when she'd like to see you again, that's probably a hint that she's doesn't want to see you, and you should stop calling her.

Best wishes!

Jerome

Discussion Questions

- How do you know at the end of one date if the person is interested in going on another date with you?

- How long should you wait to call someone for a second date?

- What kind of hints might someone give you at the end of a date that she is not interested in going on a second date?

- Why might a person say, "Sure, you can call me for a second date," if she really doesn't mean it?

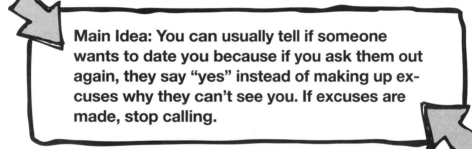

Main Idea: You can usually tell if someone wants to date you because if you ask them out again, they say "yes" instead of making up excuses why they can't see you. If excuses are made, stop calling.

Asking Her Out

Dear Haley,

I am 16 years old and really like this one girl in my class. How can I let her know that I like her without sounding like a geek and saying something like, "Maria. I like you! Pleeeeassse go out with me"?

Tony

Dear Tony,

Well, there are lots of ways that you can let someone know that you like them without actually coming out and saying those words. For example, you can do nice things for her or give her compliments such as, "You look really nice today" or "You're really fun to hang out with." She may get the hint that way.

Also, don't forget the importance of nonverbal communication (body talk). This means, for example, smiling when you see her, using good eye contact, sitting up straight and turning your body toward her so she can tell that you are listening when she talks, and nodding your head attentively.

Best wishes, and don't forget your body language communicates as much as, if not more than, your words do!

Haley

Discussion Questions

- How can you tell if someone likes you even if he or she doesn't say it with specific words?

- Give some examples of body language that's saying, "I don't care" or "I'm not listening to you." Then give examples of the opposite.

- How can you improve your nonverbal communication?

- How does it feel when someone appears to really be listening to you?

Main Idea: Let someone know you like them by using positive, verbal (speaking) and nonverbal (smiles, tone of voice, body posture) communication.

Is It O.K. to Date Someone I Met Online?

Dear Jerome,

Some of my friends have found dates in chat rooms or through other Internet services. I would like to try it, but don't know if it's a good idea or not. What do you think?

Devon

Dear Devon,

I think you are right in taking a cautious approach to meeting someone over the Internet and starting a relationship with them. While there are no doubt many innocent people just like you out there, there's always a danger that someone is not who they say they are and will try to meet you to take advantage of you.

That being said, if you still wish to use the Internet to meet someone, be sure to take precautions such as not giving away any personal information to strangers (your full name, address, and phone number) or other information that can identify you, such as what school you attend.

If you make the decision to meet face-to-face someone you've "met" over the Internet, be sure it is in a public place, preferably with another person going with you (like a good friend).

Remember to be careful out there – just because someone claims to be a certain person, he or she really is just a stranger. And even though you may have corresponded several times, it doesn't mean that you can trust them. Trust comes by knowing someone and by actual experiences with that person – not just by exchanging words!

Best wishes,

Jerome

Discussion Questions

- In what way is the Internet used to meet possible dates?

- Have you or people you know met people over the Internet (dates or friends)?

- What is the danger in having a "relationship" online?

- Where can you meet other potential dates besides the Internet?

Main Idea: If you use the Internet to meet someone, remember that person you write to is still a stranger and may not be who they claim to be. If you do choose to meet one day, always go in a group and meet in a public place.

Part Two:
Officially Dating

Are My Expectations Getting in the Way?

Dear Jerome,

Sometimes my boyfriend reacts in ways I don't expect, and I find myself disappointed. For example, if I make him a special meal and he tells me he's not that hungry, or if I get my haircut and he doesn't even notice, I get upset. Is this my problem or his?

Clara

Dear Clara,

While you would like to be acknowledged in a certain way by your boyfriend, it sounds as though this does not always happen. In general, we can't expect people to act or react the way we would like them to – it just doesn't work that way.

Your question reminds me of the old saying that there is only one person we can control: ourselves. If you are trying to control your boyfriend's reactions to things, you are not allowing him to be free to be himself around you. This will most likely lead to resentment on his part and more disappointment on your part. Try not to have an idea of what he might say or do or should say or do before it happens. That is not to say that you can't talk about your own feelings and reactions to things – you certainly can. It just means that you also need to let him have his own thoughts, feelings, and reactions separate from yours.

Best wishes!

Jerome

Discussion Questions

- Are you disappointed when others don't react the way you'd like them to?

- Do you expect people close to you to act in a certain way?

- How can you let people "be themselves"?

- What are the benefits of letting others be themselves around you?

Main Idea: We can only control our own thoughts, feelings, and emotions. We cannot control the thoughts, feelings, and emotions of others.

My Boyfriend Likes to Party

Dear Haley,

I'm dating a guy named Jim. Jim seemed really cool when I first started going out with him. We used to do a lot of stuff together on the weekends, like going to the movies or rollerblading. But recently, he's been getting more and more into partying – which I'm not – and I feel like he's pressuring me into drinking. In fact, he gets mad when he offers me something alcoholic to drink and I say no, calling me names like **"Wuss"** or **"Goody Two Shoes."** I don't know what to do. Should I break up with him?

Tammie

Dear Tammie,

It sounds to me like you and your boy-friend have a lot going on here. In my opinion, there are two serious issues to consider. One is the drinking itself; it is illegal for teens to drink. The second issue is also serious in that it appears that your boyfriend is trying to pres-sure you into doing something you are not comfortable with, and that's just plain wrong. My advice is to discuss these is-sues honestly with your boyfriend, and if things don't change, leave him for someone who is both healthy *and* respectful.

Also, name calling is just plain mean. I guess if it was me, I would have a talk with him about how he's making me feel. If he still keeps it up, I would break up with him.

Best wishes!

Haley

 # Discussion Questions

- In what situations do you see people pressuring each other?

- Is all peer pressure bad?

- When is peer pressure *not* a good thing?

- What are your views on teens and drinking?

 Main Idea: If someone is pressuring you into doing something you don't want to do, get away from them and talk to a trusted adult.

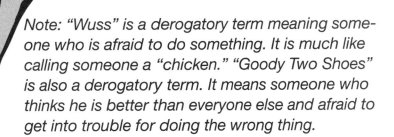 *Note: "Wuss" is a derogatory term meaning someone who is afraid to do something. It is much like calling someone a "chicken." "Goody Two Shoes" is also a derogatory term. It means someone who thinks he is better than everyone else and afraid to get into trouble for doing the wrong thing.*

I'm Meeting the Parents!

Dear Jerome,

I'm 16 years old. I'm going to be meeting my date's parents for the first time when I pick her up for a dance at school. What should I say to them?

Garth

Dear Garth,

Meeting the parents for the first time? It may seem like scary business, but it doesn't have to be.

On the night you arrive at their home, you may wish to ring the doorbell, wait for someone to answer, and then introduce yourself. Try to use the parents' formal titles, such as "Hi, Mr. and Mrs. Johnson. I'm Garth," and extend your hand for a handshake. They may ask you to call them by their first names, and this is O.K. but definitely start out with the formal address of "Mr." and "Mrs." until you're told to do otherwise. It is also polite to add, "It's nice to meet you," while shaking their hands. Also remember that when leaving, it is polite to say, "It was nice meeting you," before you walk out the door.

If they offer you something to eat or drink, it is polite to accept, even if you can only take a small portion. If they ask you to sit down for a while and talk, it is polite to do so. Also, expect that they will ask you questions such as: "Where are you going? When will you be home? Answer all questions politely, and understand that they are just making sure their daughter will be well taken care of. Assure them that she will be, and have a good time.

Best wishes!

Jerome

 # Discussion Questions

- Why can it be **nerve-wracking** to meet your date's parents?

- What makes for a good impression when meeting adults for the first time?

- What shouldn't you do when meeting someone for the first time?

- Do your parents have rules about dating?

 Main Idea: When meeting adults for the first time, it is best practice to be as polite as possible.

 Note: The term "nerve-wracking" means something that makes you very, very nervous.

Some Things About My Date Annoy Me

Dear Haley,

I've recently started dating a great guy, but he has a really annoying laugh. Some of my friends say he laughs like a donkey, and it's starting to embarrass me. Should I tell him about this?

Sheri

Dear Sheri,

It sounds to me like you've found a really great guy, who happens to have a really annoying laugh. A lot of times when dating we have to take the good with the bad. This means you put up with some annoying habits of your date, and your date puts up with some of your annoying habits. Annoyances may range from forgetting to put the toilet seat down to strange ways of acting or speaking. Many people choose to ignore minor irritations in their dates, if they can. For you, this would mean that you try not to let his laugh bother you, and that you don't bring up the fact that it bothers you.

You may be feeling bad because your friends are making the situation worse by pointing out his annoying habit and laughing at him behind his back. In this case, it would be helpful for you to make up your mind about how you're feeling about it. If you decide that it bothers you when they make fun of him, you could simply tell them, "Nobody's perfect."

Best wishes,

Haley

 # Discussion Questions

- What annoying habits bother you in others?

- What annoying habits can you ignore?

- Has anybody ever told you that you have any annoying habits?

- What is the difference between an annoying habit and a potentially harmful habit?

Main Idea: Everyone has an annoying habit. We can either choose to point it out to the person and ask him to change, or we can choose to put up with it. Remember, however, nobody's perfect!

How Can I Make It up to Her?

Dear Haley,

My girlfriend and I got into a huge argument last weekend, and I said some things I regret saying. She's really, really mad at me, and I feel horrible about it. Is there anything I can do about it now?

JaVon

Dear JaVon,

I'm sorry to hear of your argument. Unfortunately, this happens sometimes in a relationship. Often couples are able to work it out.

Since you said you're feeling badly about it and regret some of the things you said, you may want to tell your girlfriend that. Ask her to just listen if she is too upset to talk, then respectfully apologize and tell her your true feelings.

During an apology, it is usually not a good time to make excuses for what happened or to dig into the issues that caused the disagreement in the first place. Instead, it is the time to sincerely say things like, "I'm sorry. I was upset, and I didn't mean to say those things. I won't bring that up again." Everyone disagrees at some point, and most couples argue at times. Sometimes a sincere apology afterward can make the relationship even stronger.

Best wishes!

Haley

Discussion Questions

- With whom do you argue, and what do you typically argue about?

- What are some good ways to apologize?

- What else can a person do, besides saying he's sorry, to make amends after a disagreement?

- Why do couples argue in the first place?

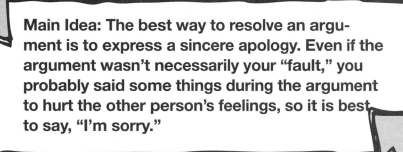

Main Idea: The best way to resolve an argument is to express a sincere apology. Even if the argument wasn't necessarily your "fault," you probably said some things during the argument to hurt the other person's feelings, so it is best to say, "I'm sorry."

Special Song

Dear Jerome,

My girlfriend wants us to have a "special song," and I don't really want one. Should I tell her that?

Wade

Dear Wade,

Unless your girlfriend picks out the theme song from "Beauty and the Beast" or something like that, it is probably not a big deal, and you may just want to let her pick one out. Choosing a special song is a common thing for girls to want to do. She is probably just thinking of sharing a special song as a kind of a secret both of you share, and this may be important to her. But if you really are bothered by the idea, you may want to tell her and perhaps think of something else to share instead. This may be a special place or a special event that you could both enjoy.

Best wishes!

Jerome

# Discussion Questions

- Why might some people make a big deal out of special songs for couples to share?

- Why might couples pick out songs for each other to express their feelings?

- Have you ever been to a wedding where the couple dances to a special song?

- Would you want to have a special song to share with someone?

Main Idea: If the person you are dating is sentimental and wants to share a special song or a special day, go along with it the best you can so you don't hurt her feelings.

Getting Possessive

Dear Haley,

I think my boyfriend is starting to get really possessive. He seems to get mad at me if I talk to other guys, or even to my close girlfriends. Usually he wants to spend time alone with me, and he gets upset if I make plans without him. At first I thought it was kind of flattering, but now it's starting to bother me. Should I be worried about this?

Mia

Dear Mia,

It sounds to me that things are out of balance with your boyfriend. In a healthy relationship, both people choose to spend time with each other and are free to talk to or spend time with others when they want to. As is the case for anything that you don't like or that doesn't feel right in a relationship, first talk to your boyfriend about it. If talking to him doesn't help and you don't know what to do about it, I suggest you confide in a trusted adult or your parents and break up with him.

Best wishes!

Haley

Discussion Questions

- What does being "possessive" of somebody mean?

- Why are some people possessive?

- Is it ever healthy to be possessive in a relationship?

- Who can you talk to if you feel like someone is being too possessive over you?

Main Idea: If your date is restricting you from spending your time the way you wish to spend it, this indicates a problem. You should tell a trusted adult and then break up if your date doesn't change.

A Birthday Present

Dear Jerome,

My girlfriend's birthday is coming up soon. I'd like to get her something nice, but I don't have much money. Should I borrow money to buy her a gift?

Enrique

Dear Enrique,

While it would be nice to get your girlfriend something expensive, and maybe even "classy," it is not necessary, especially if you can't really afford it. From my experience, most girls want to feel special, especially on their birthday. This can be done without spending a lot of cash. You could, for example, cook a special meal for her, or write a love letter to her and wrap it up in a box. Or if that's not your thing, ask her what she'd like to do on a "special date" for her birthday.

Just to clear up any possible misunderstandings, you may even wish to tell your girlfriend that you would like to do something special on her birthday, just for her, and mention that while you may be short on cash, you've got lots of other good ideas that don't involve spending money. Often hearing somebody say how much he cares means more than a fancy gift anyway.

Best wishes!

Jerome

Discussion Questions

- Is it important to spend a lot of money on gifts for someone?

- What else can you do besides spending money to show someone you care?

- What have some of your favorite presents been?

- Other than birthdays, when else might you give presents to dates?

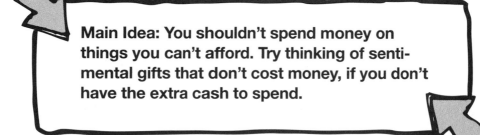

Main Idea: You shouldn't spend money on things you can't afford. Try thinking of sentimental gifts that don't cost money, if you don't have the extra cash to spend.

Someone Wants Me to Break up With My Boyfriend

Dear Haley,

There's this one guy at school who keeps telling me that I should break up with my boyfriend. My boyfriend and I get along great, and I don't even know why this other guy is getting involved. What he is doing bothers me, but I don't know what to do about it. I just wish he'd stop.

Barb

Dear Barb,

The first thing that comes to my mind in this situation is: What business is it of this other guy who you date? I think you should tell him that you will date whom-ever you wish and that he should mind his own business.

Given the fact that he is not a friend of yours, I can't help but wonder why he is even telling you this. Perhaps you could ask him why, and then after he tells you, ask him to stop it be-cause it's getting on your nerves. My guess is that perhaps he is doing it to get a reaction; perhaps he is doing it to be a **busy body**, or perhaps he is doing it because he wants you to break up with your current boyfriend and date him instead. Regard-less of his reasons, he has no right to meddle.

Now if it were your parents who had concerns about who you're dating, I would explore that with them further and ask them why they felt that way. Sometimes parents have insights that are valu-able, or they may be concerned about your well-being or safety, and those opinions should be taken into account.

In this case, however, it's fine to tell the other guy to stay out of your business!

Best wishes!

Haley

 # Discussion Questions

- Who might care about who you choose to date and why?

- Has anyone ever told you that you should break up with someone?

- Are there busy bodies out there who have opinions about who you date?

- What sorts of things about a date may concern parents?

 Main Idea: Who you choose to date is your own business in general, and if someone comments on your choice of date, you should consider who they are and why they are saying what they are saying before responding.

Note: The term "busy body" means someone who is interested in everyone else's business; a gossip.

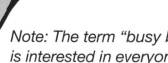

Impressing My Date

Dear Jerome,

I want to impress a girl by showing her how many sit-ups I can do because I've been working out a lot, and I'm getting good at them. Should I show her, or would that be bragging?

Duane

Dear Duane,

Yes, it would be bragging to show off how many sit-ups you can do, and it may have the opposite effect of what you intended. It sounds like you are trying to impress this girl by showing her what you're good at. Most people are not impressed with show-offs. If you really want to impress this girl, take an interest in what *she's* good at. Give her a chance to demonstrate and talk about her talents. Perhaps then, in a more natural context, you can share yours.

Best wishes,

Jerome

Discussion Questions

- Why do people want to impress others?

- How do you impress people?

- What do you think you're good at?

- How can you show or tell others what you're good at without bragging?

Main Idea: Impress someone by showing what kind of a person you are, instead of showing what you have or what you can do.

He Keeps Interrupting Me

Dear Haley,

The guy I'm dating has recently started talking at the same time I am talking, and he ends up constantly interrupting me. My friends have noticed that I get quiet around him. I guess I feel like, What's the use of talking since he does most of the talking anyway? How do I handle this?

Zehra

Dear Zehra,

It's great that your guy is into talking. However, if that means that you don't get a chance to talk even when you want to, that can be a problem. Tell him how this is making you feel, and then ask him politely to let you have a chance to talk in conversations as well. If he interrupts again in the middle of a conversation, gently point it out to him, because he may not realize that he's doing it.

If he still doesn't stop, and you feel like your voice is not being heard, you may start to feel angry and neglected. You deserve to be an equal partner who is treated with respect; if he can't do that, perhaps you should consider breaking up with him.

Best wishes!

Haley

Discussion Questions

- Why do people interrupt others?

- How does it feel when you get interrupted?

- What would an ideal conversation sound like?

- What does it mean to be treated as an "equal partner?"

Main Idea: Both people in a dating relationship should be allowed time to be listened to as well as time to speak.

Wanting to Slow It Down

Dear Haley,

The guy I've started dating is really fun to be around, but he seems too interested in kissing me. I mean, I like him, but I want to take it slow. Obviously he doesn't, and I'm feeling pressured. What should I do?

Sandra

Dear Sandra,

I think you need to have an honest discussion with this guy. Tell him what your expectations are and be clear about what you want and don't want. Also, realize that your nonverbal communication – smiling, hugging, touching – sends a "message" similar to words. If you wish for a specific type of physical intimacy, make sure to make it clear with both your body and your words. The danger is that if you don't say and mean "no" clearly – with both your body and your words – the message that you are sending can be misinterpreted. Remember though, you ALWAYS have the right to choose your actions with your body, and you also have the right to stop intimacy any time you wish. If that's not acceptable to him, that means he doesn't respect your wishes. Then it's time to talk to a trusted adult about the situation, and to break up with him.

Best wishes!

Haley

# Discussion Questions

- Have you ever been with someone who has different physical expectations than you do?

- When does unwanted touch become harmful?

- What should you do if someone tries to force you to kiss him or her?

- Who can you talk to if you feel your date is pressuring you?

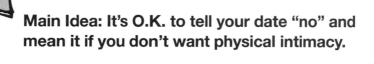

Main Idea: It's O.K. to tell your date "no" and mean it if you don't want physical intimacy.

Standing up for Me too Much

Dear Jerome,

My boyfriend is always trying to stick up for me, even if I don't want him to. For example, if someone says something to me that he doesn't like, he either tells them to shut up, or he wants to fight.

I tried to tell him that I can stand up for myself and don't need his "help," but he doesn't seem to listen. It's really starting to embarrass me! What do you recommend?

Tannika

Dear Tannika,

It sounds like your boyfriend has been watching too many action/drama movies where the man saves the woman from some sort of danger and walks away the hero. Another possibility is that he is crossing boundary lines and becoming either possessive over you or confusing others' comments to you for comments being made to him.

My advice to you is to use your skills in assertion and talk to him about what's bothering you. You may wish to use "I" statements. Using an "I" statement means that you state what is bothering you from your point of view, starting with, "I feel _____ when you _____." The reason this is a good idea in general is that it doesn't make the other person feel defensive. On the other hand, if, for example, you said, "You bother me when you act like _____," the other person may feel angry and hurt and may say something rude back.

Using "I" statements instead of "you" statements allows you to be assertive in a non-threatening manner. In this case, you may wish to say something like: "I feel embarrassed when you try to defend me because I know how to stand up for myself. From now on I would like you to let me handle people's comments and ask you for help only when I need it." If your boyfriend still doesn't listen and respect your wishes, talk to a trusted adult and consider breaking up with him.

Best wishes,

Jerome

Discussion Questions

- When might you wish **to stick up for** a date?

- Do you need to react to all comments made to you or a date?

- How can you tell if your date is starting to become possessive?

- How can two people work it out if one of them feels the other is being picked on?

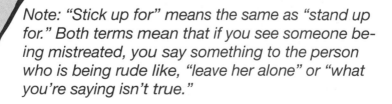

Main Idea: If you don't want your date to do something, assert yourself by using "I" statements. If she doesn't respect you, break up with her.

Note: "Stick up for" means the same as "stand up for." Both terms mean that if you see someone being mistreated, you say something to the person who is being rude like, "leave her alone" or "what you're saying isn't true."

Nosey Friend

Dear Haley,

My friend keeps asking me to tell her about my dates in detail – like if my boyfriend is a good kisser and stuff like that. She's kind of lonely, and I want to be nice to her, but I think her questions are too personal. What should I tell her?

Michele

Dear Michele,

Have you ever heard the expression, "What happens in Vegas stays in Vegas?" This means that some things you do are meant to be kept private. This could also be the standard for dating, meaning that what you do and say on a date should stay between you and the person you're dating.

Nevertheless, there are situations where you want to share what happens on a date. Examples may be if you have questions about what's appropriate and what is not on a date, if you are feeling uncomfortable in a dating situation, or if your date shares with you something that may hurt you or him (you need to be able to share this information with a trusted adult). In those cases, talking about it IS the right thing to do!

In your current situation, your friend appears to be prying into your personal life, and this really is none of her business – lonely or not. It would be best to tell her politely, "I don't **kiss and tell**" and leave it at that!

Best wishes!

Haley

Discussion Questions

- Do you know anyone who "kisses and tells"?

- How might sharing personal details of a date with others damage your relationship?

- What are some examples of what is private or public about your relationship?

- In which situations *should* you tell another person about what happens on your dates?

Main Idea: Some details of your dates such as personal conversation or touch should remain between you and your date. There are situations, however, such as when you are questioning whether or not something is appropriate, when you should talk to a trusted adult about what happens on your date.

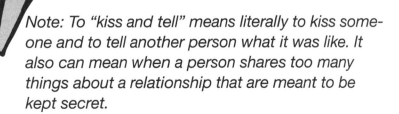

Note: To "kiss and tell" means literally to kiss someone and to tell another person what it was like. It also can mean when a person shares too many things about a relationship that are meant to be kept secret.

Is Dating Competitive?

Dear Jerome,

It seems like a lot of the popular guys date a lot and switch girlfriends often. Is it O.K. to do that?

Derrick

Dear Derrick,

While it may seem that dating is a competition to some, the goal of dating shouldn't be just to date as many people as possible so that you can brag about it to friends later. This is much different from having a true relationship with someone you care about and is nowhere nearly as fulfilling.

Some people choose to do this, and even worse, some people try to go out with another person just to get someone they really like jealous. I know it doesn't make a lot of sense, but some people will do anything to get noticed – and that includes hurting others' feelings, unfortunately.

Best wishes!

Jerome

 # Discussion Questions

- Why might someone want to date as many people as possible?

- Have you observed anyone who tries to make others jealous? If so, how?

- What are the characteristics of a caring relationship?

- How can you avoid people who don't want a sincere relationship with you?

Main Idea: Some people want to date others, not because they want a relationship with them, but to brag about going out with them or to make someone else jealous.

Bothered by His Friend

Dear Haley,

My boyfriend, Parker, has a really annoying friend named Connor. I can't stand to be around Connor but feel forced into it because Parker wants to spend time with him as well as with me. When I tell him, he says there's nothing wrong with Connor, and that I should be more open-minded. Should I be?

Nancy

Dear Nancy,

In a perfect world, your friend's friend would be your friend as well. But in reality, it doesn't always work that way. Connor is Parker's friend because he chose him as his friend. You didn't.

In dating situations, this can be a bit tricky. Generally speaking, you should tolerate Connor to a certain extent, out of respect for Parker. However, if Connor starts to bother you in a way that is more than just annoying habits – for example, if he starts to "butt into" your relationship with Parker such as by offering advice that neither you nor Parker asks for, or by wanting to be too much of a part of your relationship – then it is time to talk to Parker about working something out.

It may turn out that the two of you decide that while Parker can still be friends with Connor, you will do something else during the time they are together, such as spending time with your own close friends.

Best wishes!

Haley

Discussion Questions

- Have you ever disliked one of your date's friends? How did you handle it?

- How can you "tolerate" a person, even if you really don't like him?

- Do you expect that everyone will like whom you choose to be friends with?

- What could you say to your date if they had a friend who was interfering with your relationship?

Main Idea: It is generally expected that you should tolerate your date's friends unless they interfere with your relationship.

Wishing for Perfection

Dear Jerome,

When I go out with a girl, I want it to be the perfect situation. In my mind, this means that we go to fun places, she laughs at my jokes, and we never argue. Is this possible?

Vic

Dear Vic,

To answer your question, no it's not possible, at least not on a regular basis. What you have just described is an ideal situation. Who wouldn't want that? But the reality is that it just doesn't happen, and to think that it might will only set you up for disappointment.

That's not to say that you won't go on some really awesome dates. It's also not to say that you won't get along great with whomever you're dating and that you can't work through conflicts and really enjoy each other's company. This type of situation is potentially not only attainable, but if you work hard and work together with the right person, there's a good chance that it *will* happen.

Best wishes!

Jerome

Discussion Questions

- What would your ideal girlfriend or boyfriend be like?

- What would your ideal relationship be like?

- What's realistic to expect when dating? Why?

- Can you be happy with the way things are, instead of the way you want things to be?

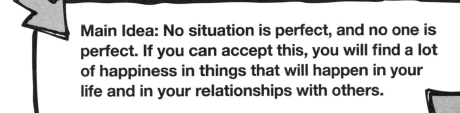

Main Idea: No situation is perfect, and no one is perfect. If you can accept this, you will find a lot of happiness in things that will happen in your life and in your relationships with others.

Only Doing What He Wants to Do

Dear Haley,

I spend a lot of time on dates doing things that my boyfriend wants to do, like going to movies and parties. When I ask him to do things that I like to do, he always makes an excuse for why he can't do them. He also doesn't want me to do anything without him, so I'm feeling stuck. What should I do?

Val

Dear Val,

Ideally, the best dates are those in which each person enjoys the date equally. But the reality is that people's interests vary, and one person in the relationship or date ends up getting to do more of what he or she wants to do than the other.

When things become out of balance, and one person seems to *always* get to do the preferred activity, that's when problems can start. I suggest that you talk honestly about this issue with your boyfriend. Tell him your feelings about what's happening and offer some suggestions for what changes to make. For example, if you always go to movies and parties but would also like to go hiking, try setting up some specific dates to do both.

If your boyfriend doesn't want to take you up on it, try coming up with something completely different that you might *both* enjoy. If he still doesn't take your wishes into consideration, it may indicate a larger issue, such as he wishes to control the relationship. This would indicate that the relationship is out of balance, and you should talk to a trusted adult and consider breaking up with him.

Best wishes!

Haley

Discussion Questions

- Is it O.K. for people who are dating to do things separately occasionally?

- How might a person feel if she rarely gets to do the things she wants to do on dates?

- How can you tell if someone is starting to be controlling?

- Who can you talk to if you feel like your relationship is out of balance?

Main Idea: If your date continually refuses to take your wishes into consideration, think about breaking up with him, because it isn't healthy.

Table Manners

Dear Jerome,

My girlfriend says I eat like a pig, and it grosses her out. It seems to me that she wants me to eat like her and be ultra polite at the dinner table. What should I say to her?

Greg

Dear Greg,

Since your girlfriend suggested rather strongly that your eating habits need improvement, I have some basic suggestions for you. While dining in public, it is appropriate to chew food slowly with your mouth closed, pass food politely, and take reasonable portions. It's *never* cool to reach across someone for a dish, or to stuff as much as you can into your mouth like you are starving.

While you don't have to overdo it in the etiquette department, it is polite to follow basic eating rules so that other people are not, in your girlfriend's words, "grossed out." Tell her you'll work on it and truly try!

Best wishes!

Jerome

Discussion Questions

- What types of things are important for you to keep in mind while eating with others?

- Do you use good etiquette while eating? If so, why or why not?

- Is it O.K. to "eat like a pig" when you're alone?

- What are other examples of polite behavior on a date besides good table manners?

Main Idea: When eating out in public, don't make any unnecessary noises that draw attention to you.

Still Upset after an Argument

Dear Jerome,

My girlfriend and I had a really intense argument last week. I am "over it" and I said I'm sorry, but now she's acting all weird around me, like she's mad at me or something. What's going on here?

Dale

Dear Dale,

While it sounds as though you are "over" the conflict you had, perhaps your girlfriend is not, and that may be why she is acting the way she is. While I don't know what is going on in her head, here are some possibilities that immediately come to my mind: Perhaps her feelings are still hurt; perhaps there are still some unresolved issues that you need to work through as a couple; perhaps the argument has changed your relationship somehow in her mind.

The fact is, right now you don't know what she's thinking, but you can tell by the way she's acting that something's wrong. The best thing to do in this situation is to talk to your girlfriend about what she's feeling. Perhaps you could start out by telling her, in a non-threatening sort of way, what you've noticed specifically about the way she's been acting and then ask if there's anything that you can do to help. The only way you'll really know what's going on is by talking with her about her feelings.

Best wishes!

Jerome

Discussion Questions

- Have you ever gotten into a really bad argument with someone you were dating?

- How do you usually "make up" after an argument?

- Why might one person still be upset after an argument, even after the other has said she was sorry?

- Do you **forgive and forget**?

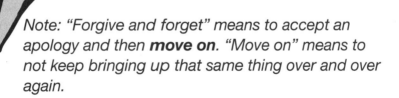

Main Idea: If you notice that your date's behavior is changing, tell her about your observations and ask if there's anything you can do to help.

*Note: "Forgive and forget" means to accept an apology and then **move on**. "Move on" means to not keep bringing up that same thing over and over again.*

How Can I Tell if Things Are Getting Serious?

Dear Haley,

My boyfriend and I have been dating for about eight weeks. How can I tell if this is a serious relationship or not?

Bethany

Dear Bethany,

Some relationships are casual, meaning that two people date one another on occasion, or just in groups, and don't consider each other boyfriend and girlfriend. In more serious relationships, two people decide to date one another and no one else, they often share intimate thoughts such as their true thoughts and feelings about things, and they generally try to please one another by showing genuine care and concern for one another.

The two of you will decide whether this is either a casual or a more serious relationship. The key is to talk to each other about what each of you wants.

Best wishes!

Haley

 # Discussion Questions

- What do you think are the characteristics of a casual relationship?

- What do you think are the characteristics of a more serious relationship?

- What happens when two people who are dating have different ideas about what kind of relationship to have?

- What happen in the best possible situation when deciding how serious the relationship is?

Main Idea: Both people in a relationship need to decide and agree on how serious they want the relationship to be.

Dating Two People at the Same Time

Dear Jerome,

I am going out with a girl, but I am considering dating someone else, too. Would that be cheating?

Anthony

Dear Anthony,

Unless you and your girl have a special arrangement in which you can see other people, what you described would be considered cheating. Cheating basically means that one person trusts another person not to do something – like being with someone else instead of them – and they do it anyway. Cheating also implies that you are **going behind someone's back** and trying to deceive him or her and get away with it.

My advice to you is to either talk to your girlfriend about dating other people while dating her, or date someone else *instead* of your girlfriend. You really can't have it both ways without someone's feelings getting hurt.

Best wishes!

Jerome

Discussion Questions

- What does it mean to be a "two-timer"?

- Do you know anyone who has cheated in a relationship? What happened?

- Is it still cheating if you don't get caught?

- If a person is tempted to cheat, what's the right thing to do?

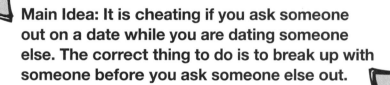

Main Idea: It is cheating if you ask someone out on a date while you are dating someone else. The correct thing to do is to break up with someone before you ask someone else out.

Note: To "go behind someone's back" means doing something without telling the other person, usually in a selfish and dishonest way. The expressions "two timing," "double dipping," and being a "player" refer to dating more than one person at the same time.

Is It Over?

Dear Haley,

My boyfriend and I have been dating for about six months. Lately he's been acting distant; he makes up excuses why he can't see me very often and says that he wants to spend more time with his friends. Should I be worried that he wants to break up?

Mary Ellen

Dear Mary Ellen,

My advice to you is to talk to your boyfriend and ask him how he feels about the relationship. There may be a reason why he is making excuses not to see you, and you deserve to know what he's thinking, even though it may not be what you want to hear.

In general, there are signs that a relationship may be in trouble, meaning someone may wish to break up soon. Some of the signs include not wishing to spend as much time together, wanting to spend time with others, not having much fun together, no longer being interested in each other's thoughts or concerns, and finding faults with one another.

And even though your boyfriend is showing signs of possibly wanting to break up, it doesn't mean that it is certain to happen. Ask him what he's thinking and go from there.

Best Wishes!

Haley

 # Discussion Questions

- What are some signs that you've noticed when someone wants to break up with you?

- Why might your boyfriend or girlfriend ignore you instead of admitting there's a problem in the relationship?

- What can you do, if anything, when someone appears to be growing distant?

- Why might someone not want to tell you that they want to break up with you?

Main Idea: If you notice some of the signs of breaking up, ask your boyfriend or girlfriend what they are thinking.

Another Girl Called Me, and My Girlfriend Got Mad

Dear Jerome,

A girl from my class called my house to talk to me and get my girlfriend's phone number so that they could do something some time. My girlfriend found out about it and got really, really angry. Did I do something wrong?

Eric

Dear Eric,

It sounds to me that your girlfriend got jealous because she felt that the other girl was interested in dating you. Even though you didn't consciously do anything wrong, the situation could have been greatly improved with communication. For example, when the other girl called, you could have asked her to talk to your girlfriend at school and ask her for her number. Or you could have told the other girl that you'd have to ask your girlfriend if she wanted you to give out her number. The bottom line is, in general, don't give out others' phone numbers without their permission.

It sounds to me like this was a pretty honest mistake, and if you have a trusting relationship with your girlfriend, she will most likely understand.

Best wishes!

Jerome

 # Discussion Questions

- Is it O.K. to call someone at home if he or she has a girlfriend or boyfriend?

- How do you know when it's O.K. to give someone's phone number out?

- Would you mind if someone gave your phone number to someone else?

- Why is good communication important in a relationship?

Main Idea: Never give out anyone's private information – such as a phone number or address – without getting permission from the other person to do so.

Picking a Fight

Dear Jerome,

Last night I started an argument with my girlfriend. I was upset with something she did last week that really bugged me, but we never really talked about it. I feel bad about it today, and I keep apologizing for it, but it's like she doesn't even want to talk to me. Is there anything I can do at this point? I feel awful!

Joseph

Dear Joseph,

It sounds to me as if there are two things going on here. Number one, there is a communication issue. Communication is probably the most important aspect of a relationship: being able to truly talk and listen to one another even if you disagree, or if the subject matter is difficult to talk about. Number two, it sounds as if you hurt your girlfriend's feelings by getting into the argument in the first place. I know you said that you were sorry, but she may still be upset and need time to forgive you.

The best thing you can do is to take steps to improve your communication by practicing listening to your date and asking questions about how she is feeling while putting your own feelings aside for the moment. After you think you understand her point of view, then and only then, should you interject yours. While this may sound easy, it is difficult to do. If you can master it, however, you can both improve your communication and avoid needless arguments.

Best wishes!

Jerome

# Discussion Questions

- Have you ever **blown up** at someone close to you over something minor, when in reality you were upset about something else? If so, give an example.

- How do you usually react when you are angry?

- What would really good communication look like in a relationship?

- What are the benefits of good communication?

Main Idea: The key to good communication is good listening. The key to good listening is trying to truly understand what the other person is saying and feeling.

Note: "Blown up" in this case means that you got very angry and possibly caused a scene.

Anger Issues

Dear Haley,

I have a problem. I get really, really angry, sometimes even over little stuff, and I feel I'm losing it when I get stressed. This is causing problems with my boyfriend, because sometimes I yell or punch walls for what appears to be no good reason.

I don't want to be like this. Is there any hope for me?

Jenny

Dear Jenny,

It sounds like you have some issues with anger that you need to deal with in order to have healthy relationships.

The first step, which you've already taken, is to recognize that you need to change. Most good anger management strategies include understanding why you react emotionally (what your triggers are and what is going on in your head) and using alternatives to deal with stress more effectively (such as taking deep breaths, counting to 10, walking away, talking through the situation when you are more calm, etc.).

You may also consider talking to a professional, such as a counselor at school, about this. School counselors often offer good resources. You're not alone in this, and the good news is that if you can become healthier, your relationship will also become healthier.

Best wishes!

Haley

 # Discussion Questions

- How do you handle your anger?

- How could you better handle your anger?

- Who are some good role models are out there for you regarding handling stress?

- What are some good ways for you to handle stress when you start to feel angry?

Main Idea: Learn good ways to deal with anger and anxiety by talking to a professional if you need to.

Deciding Whether or Not to Have Sex

Dear Jerome,

My girlfriend and I are deciding whether or not to have sex. We're talking a lot about it and trying to make sure that we are both ready for it. What sorts of things should we consider?

Sean

Dear Sean,

The decision about whether or not to have sex is a very personal one that depends a lot on your own values as well as the values of your girlfriend. This decision is very important in a relationship, and it is good to hear that you are giving it a lot of thought and are talking through things.

While there are many factors to consider, here are some of the major ones that immediately come to mind and that may be useful in your discussions:

- Does each of you feel "ready" to have sex?

- Do you both have all the information you need? (Information on protection, pregnancy, potential sexually transmitted diseases, etc.)

- Does having sex align with your personal values?

- Do you each have trusted adults you can go to for guidance and information?

The decision about having sex is a very important one. Take your time and consider all your options, including abstinence, which means choosing NOT to have sex. Also, try to keep in mind that if you are feeling pressure to have sex, or if one person wants to have sex and the other doesn't, or if you want to have sex just because you've heard a lot about it, that should be telling you to make the decision to *wait* to have sex because you are not ready as a couple.

Best wishes!

Jerome

Discussion Questions

- What values should be considered when a couple thinks about having sex?

- Where can you get information about sex?

- Why might couples choose abstinence?

- Who can you talk to about sex?

Main Idea: Think carefully about the many aspects of having sex before you make your decision to either have sex or not to have sex – it's a very important decision that can affect the rest of your life.

May I Kiss You?

Dear Jerome,

I'm going on a date on Saturday night with a girl I've taken out several times before. We've been getting along great, and I think she likes me. Here's the thing: I really want to kiss her, but I'm not sure how she'll react. What should I do?

Alex

Dear Alex,

Well, first off, I'd like to say that this really is a big deal, because what you are talking about is becoming physically close with this girl. She may or may not want that, so I'm glad you asked. I think that if you are unsure how your date will react when you try to kiss her, ask her before you do it.

While it never hurts to ask, in this case it may be the only way for you to know what she wants. A girl may even find it flattering and very polite if you say something like, "I'd really like to kiss you. Is that O.K. with you?"

Best wishes!

Jerome

# Discussion Questions

- Why is it important to check with the person before you kiss her or become physically close with her?

- What might happen if you try to kiss someone who doesn't want to be kissed?

- What are some good ways to ask to kiss someone?

- What can you say if the person says, "No, I really don't want that kind of relationship"?

Main Idea: Ask before you become physically close to your date.

Part Three: When It's Over

Is It O.K. to Break up Over the Phone?

Dear Jerome,

My relationship with my girlfriend of six months is basically over. When we're together, we argue all the time, and we don't seem to have much in common any more. Should I break up with her face-to-face, or can I just leave a message on her voice mail? I'm afraid that if I tell her in person, she'll start yelling and crying in public!

Troy

Dear Troy,

In general, the correct (and most difficult!) thing to do is to break up in person. In your case, you may wish to break up in a public place such as a restaurant or coffee shop.

Of course, there may be situations where it is best to NOT to see the person at all, such as when there is concern for your personal safety. In a case like that, breaking up either by telephone or by email are acceptable alternatives. If you do find yourself in a situation like this, be sure to seek the assistance of a trusted adult.

Best wishes,

Jerome

 # Discussion Questions

- Why is it hard to end relationships?

- What are some reasons why people break up?

- How would you like someone to break up with you? (If she was going to anyway, that is!)

- What are some situations in which it is better NOT to see the person face-to-face when breaking up?

Main Idea: When a relationship is over, break up with the person face-to-face, whenever possible, unless there are safety concerns or other important issues.

How Do I Tell Him to Give Me My Space?

Dear Haley,

I have kind of liked this one guy for a while, but now things aren't going that well. It turns out that we don't have as much in common as I first thought, and he actually really annoys me. However, he thinks we're going out, and he wants to see me more than I want to see him. How do I tell him to **back off** without hurting his feelings?

Josie

Dear Josie,

First, I think it's very thoughtful of you to think of how to distance yourself from this guy without making him feel bad. But the truth is that there may be no good way to **get your own space** without him feeling bad about it.

You do have some options. You could simply stop returning his calls or even talking to him. But that might confuse him and make him want to contact you even more to find out what's going on. Another option is to tell him honestly that, while he's a nice guy, you don't feel the same way he does, and you need some space. Yet another way to approach it is to say some nice, truthful things about him and then tell him why you no longer wish to spend a lot of time with him.

While there is no easy way to avoid hurting someone's feelings, to continue spending time with him because it makes him feel good can only lead to your own frustration and resentment of him. And, in the long run, it's not fair to either of you.

Best wishes!

Haley

Discussion Questions

- Why might someone wish to spend a lot of time with you, even though you don't appear to want to spend time with him?

- Why is it hard to reject another person?

- What are some ways you could ask for your own space?

- What kind of people do you wish to spend your time with?

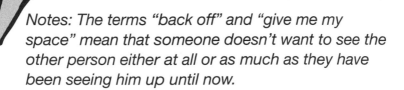

Main Idea: If he wants to spend more time with you than you want to spend with him, it is best to tell him about the way you feel about it honestly, even though it may hurt his feelings.

Notes: The terms "back off" and "give me my space" mean that someone doesn't want to see the other person either at all or as much as they have been seeing him up until now.

Can I Date My Friend's Ex?

Dear Jerome,

My best friend just broke up with his girlfriend, Kristina. I think she's really attractive. Is it O.K. to ask her out?

Taylor

Dear Taylor,

While the choice of who to date is always a personal decision, I think it is wise to think carefully about this one. Perhaps you are thinking, "Kristina is a great girl. I can see why my friend went out with her. Now he no longer wants to date her, and I do, so what's the problem?"

Well, it may be a problem if your friend doesn't see things that way. For example, your friend may be thinking, "There are plenty of other girls to date. Why would Taylor pick someone I just broke up with? Does he see this as a competition?" He also may be worried that you two will talk about him in a personal way, like if Kristina shares some of the secrets he told her. He may also still be hurt over the relationship, and he may not want to be reminded of it every time he sees you two together.

Of course, it could be the case that your friend is O.K. with this, but if he is not, you may risk losing him as a friend. As a general rule, most people try to avoid dating their friend's **exes**, at least right away, just because of the potential damage it may cause. My advice to you is to weigh your options carefully.

Best wishes,

Jerome

 # Discussion Questions

- Would you ever date a friend's ex? Why or why not?

- Do you think timing plays a role in dating someone's ex?

- What does it mean when somebody says, "There are plenty of fish in the sea"?

- How would you feel if your friend dated your ex?

 Main Idea: Although it works out in some cases, it is generally not acceptable to date your friend's ex.

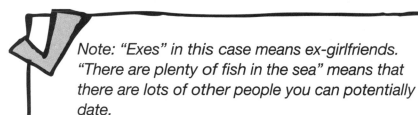 *Note: "Exes" in this case means ex-girlfriends. "There are plenty of fish in the sea" means that there are lots of other people you can potentially date.*

Can We Still Be Friends?

Dear Haley,

My boyfriend broke up with me a couple of weeks ago; things just weren't working out between us. He told me that he still wanted to be friends. However, now he wants nothing to do with me and avoids talking to me or taking my phone calls. Why did he even bother saying that he wanted to stay friends?

Kari

Dear Kari,

It appears to me that your boyfriend has used a common break-up line to end the relationship. When someone is breaking up with you and says, "Let's be friends," it generally means that he is trying to break up with you in a polite way so that your feelings don't get too hurt. What it really means is this: "Our relationship has changed, and I won't be seeing you any more."

Other common break-up lines, used for the same reason, are "It's not you, it's me." Or "I'm just not ready for this kind of relationship."

There are cases in which people who once dated remain friends. When that happens, it usually doesn't happen right away, however. Don't despair, though. Just because the situation is awkward right now does not mean it will stay that way. In the meantime, since he appears not to want to hang out with you, try spending time with other friends, or doing the things that you really like to do to get your mind off of the break-up.

Best wishes!

Haley

 # Discussion Questions

- Have you (or anyone you know) ever said to you, "We can still be friends" when her intention was really to break up?

- Why do people often soften the break-up, instead of simply saying, "I don't want to go out with you any more?"

- What might be some polite things to say when you break up with someone?

Main Idea: Sometimes when someone breaks up with you by saying, "We can still be friends," he is just being polite and really doesn't want to see you any more. If he truly wants to be friends after the break-up, he will call you.

I Still "Like" My Ex

Dear Jerome,

My girlfriend Tina broke up with me six months ago. I still really like her, though, and start to feel jealous when I'm around and see other guys talking to her. We are just friends (her decision), and I don't think we'll ever get back together. So why am I acting like this?

Ken

Dear Ken,

Wow! This is a hard situation. It sounds as if you still like Tina, but she may not feel the same way about you. Number one, I think it's important to realize that this is a tough feeling; it's called "rejection." In a perfect world, everyone who dates would like each other equally. But the reality is that this does not always happen, and if you break up, it's definitely not happening. It hurts, though, and perhaps it's that hurt feeling that's showing up now as jealousy when another guy talks to your former girlfriend.

My advice is to spend less time hanging out with Tina and *less time thinking about her,* even though you still like her and may want to see her often. Right away, you may wish to intentionally try not to think about her and spend time with other friends or family, or do things like go to the movies or play sports and video games to help you get your mind off of her and get through this. With time, you may be able to have a friendship with her without hurt feelings, but it sounds like you're just not there yet, and that's O.K. You deserve some time to heal.

Best wishes!

Jerome

Discussion Questions

- Have you ever liked someone more than he or she liked you? What happened?

- Has anyone ever liked you more than you liked the person? What happened?

- What makes you feel jealous?

- What distracts you when you want to get your mind off of something?

Main Idea: The best thing to do after a break-up is to keep busy so you don't think of the person so much.

We Broke up, and I Feel Lousy

Dear Jerome,

I just broke up with my girlfriend, and I'm really, really **bummed out.** How long will this last, and will I ever want to date anyone else again?

Mike

Dear Mike,

Sorry to hear about your situation. Breaking up can be painful and often takes a while to recover from. It's no wonder that there are so many songs that have to do with the pain of breaking up with someone. The truth is, it hurts!

While there is no set time for how long it takes to recover from a break-up, eventually the pain does lessen, and things do get better. In the meantime, it may be helpful for you to hang out with friends and spend some time doing the things you like to do and that make you feel good instead of dwelling on your loss. You may also wish to avoid the places where your ex-girlfriend hangs until you feel you are ready to see her again.

My guess is that eventually you will start to date again. For right now, however, this stinks!

Best wishes,

Jerome

Discussion Questions

- What are some reasons why people break up with each other?

- Have you ever been through a bad break-up? If so, what happened?

- If you were hurt in a break-up, what might help you feel better?

- How can you help a friend out who's going through a break-up?

Main Idea: It hurts to break up with someone, but you will start to feel better in time, especially if you focus on the things you like to do instead of focusing on your feelings of sadness.

Note: "Bummed out" means feeling bad about something.

Part Four:
Just Wondering ...

Is It Weird NOT to Date?

Dear Haley,

I am 16 years old and I really don't feel like dating, even though a lot of my friends already are. Am I weird?

Teresa

Dear Teresa,

First, you are not "weird" for choosing not to date! Dating is a very personal decision and should be made when, and if, you are ready. I know that as a teenager, it often seems that "everyone is dating," but if you look around, that's not always the case.

You may very well find that instead of spending your time dating, you are spending it learning about yourself, learning new skills, or focusing on other relationships such as with family or friends. These are also very good uses of time and shouldn't be overlooked because of pressure to date.

Best wishes!

Haley

 # Discussion Questions

- What sorts of pressures to date exist for teen-agers?

- Why might someone choose not to date?

- What does it mean to date anyway?

- If you choose not to date, what sorts of things would you do instead?

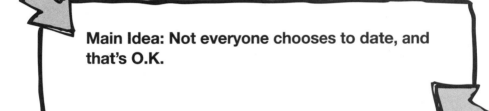

Main Idea: Not everyone chooses to date, and that's O.K.

Attractiveness

Dear Haley,

I'm a 16-year-old girl with blond hair and brown eyes. My friends say I'm cute, but I'm not so sure. How do I know if I'm attractive?

Carla

Dear Carla,

I guess my question to you would be: "Do you think you're cute?" I ask this question because it seems that 99% of being attractive is *feeling* attractive. To me, this means feeling good about myself and taking good care of my body by eating right and exercising. When you feel good on the inside, it automatically shines through on the outside.

Generally, people who feel good about themselves appear confident and more attractive than those who don't. Of course, if you would like to change something about your appearance because it would make you feel better about yourself, you could try to find a haircut that suits you, shed a few pounds if necessary, or try a new outfit. However, if you think you look good "as is," you probably do!

Best wishes,

Haley

Discussion Questions

- What makes another person attractive to you?

- What type of person are you attracted to?

- Is the old saying really true: "It's what's on the inside that counts"?

- What kind of images are in your mind when you think of beautiful people?

- Can anyone be beautiful? Why or why not?

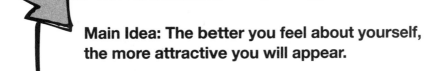

Main Idea: The better you feel about yourself, the more attractive you will appear.

Am I Gay?

Dear Jerome,

Lately I find myself attracted to other guys. A few guys I know are really cool and good-looking, and I like hanging around them. Could I be gay?

Mark

Dear Mark,

Well, first of all, it is very natural to be attracted to all sorts of people, and some of those people may very well happen to be of the same sex as you. This does not necessarily mean that you are gay, as many people experience homosexual thoughts without actually being gay.

If it does end up that you are indeed gay, it may prove to be another aspect of who you are that you are discovering. In this case, you may wish to discuss your new discoveries with an adult you can trust. While not all people are open to the idea of homosexuality, many are. The trick is to find out who the people are in your life who will accept you and love you for who you are, not just who they want you to be.

Best wishes!

Jerome

 # Discussion Questions

- What kind of sexual thoughts are considered "natural"?

- What do people say about the issue of homo-sexuality?

- What are your views of homosexuality?

- How would you react if someone rejected you because of who you were?

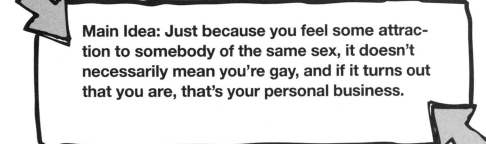

Main Idea: Just because you feel some attraction to somebody of the same sex, it doesn't necessarily mean you're gay, and if it turns out that you are, that's your personal business.

How Can I Learn More About Dating?

Dear Haley,

I don't know much about dating, or even if I want to try it at this point. How can I find out more about it without actually doing it myself?

Lexi

Dear Lexi,

If you'd like to study up on dating, you're in luck because there is a lot of information out there for teenagers. For example, you can look up "Teens and Dating" on the Internet, rent movies about teenage romance, and buy teen magazines. These all have things to say about dating and have the potential to help you learn about dating. For example, you could watch an old movie like *Pretty in Pink,* and analyze the way the characters relate to each other and how they are feeling. The thing to watch out for, however, is that most of these sources are not out there just to inform, but to entertain – which means they may not portray reality but "idealized" situations. Or they might be trying to sell products. For example, magazines may wish to encourage you to buy a certain type of music or clothing, under the disguise of talking about dating and teen romance. Choose your information wisely and when in doubt, ask for advice from somebody you trust.

Best wishes!

Haley

 # Discussion Questions

- Where do you think some good sources are to learn about dating?

- What are some common themes out there about teens and dating?

- Why do you have to be careful about believing everything you read in a magazine or on the Internet, or watch in a movie?

- Do you have any favorite "romance" movies?

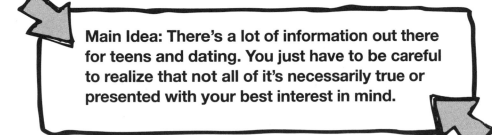

Main Idea: There's a lot of information out there for teens and dating. You just have to be careful to realize that not all of it's necessarily true or presented with your best interest in mind.

Is It O.K. to Be in Love with My Teacher?

Dear Jerome,

I am in love with my history teacher. She is totally pretty, and she makes learning history fun. She also makes special time for me to talk about assignments and gives me extra help whenever I need it. Sometimes I dream that she's my girlfriend. Is that normal?

Darrin

Dear Darrin,

It sounds like your history teacher has some real outstanding qualities. And no, I don't think you're weird! It's perfectly normal to like someone you find attractive, intelligent, and who makes you feel good when you're around them. This is often called **having a crush** on someone. A crush can get to be a problem, however, if you tell her your true feelings about her, because it might make her feel uncomfortable as your teacher. It would also be a problem for a high school teacher to date a student; there are laws against that. So for now I would say, enjoy the private thoughts you have and appreciate the fact that you have an awesome teacher who also happens to be very attractive!

Best wishes!

Jerome

 # Discussion Questions

- Have you ever had a crush on a teacher?

- What might cause someone to fall in love with his or her teacher?

- Why do you think there are laws against people in authority (teachers, police officers, etc.) dating people who are supposed to be working for them?

- What would happen if teachers started dating students?

Main Idea: While it is normal for students to have an occasional crush on a teacher, it is unethical for teachers in schools to date students.

Note: "Having a crush" on someone means that you like them in a romantic sort of way.

Will I Ever Go on a Date?

Dear Haley,

It seems like everywhere I go – school, the mall, wherever – I see other teenagers dating and having a great time. I've never even been on a date and am starting to wonder if anyone will ever ask me out.

Is there any hope for me?

Anna

Dear Anna,

I would agree that in today's world, it may seem that everyone is dating. You see it all around you, especially on TV and in movies and magazines. But the truth of the matter is that right now, as you read this, there are plenty of other teens who are also not dating for various reasons.

It sounds to me as if you'd like to date but are not currently doing so. Perhaps you could go out with groups of friends with the idea that you may meet other teenagers who are also interested in dating. Ideas for this include going to the movies, roller-skating, dances, sporting events, etc.

Another good way to meet people is to join a club or an extra-curricular activity. And don't forget, you can always ask someone out instead of waiting to be asked. Try not to be discouraged, however, if there are some disappointments along the way such as being turned down for a date. This happens to everyone, and you just have to pick yourself up and try again!

Best wishes,

Haley

 # Discussion Questions

- Where are good places to meet people who you may wish to date?

- What other fun things can you do with your time instead of dating?

- What might happen if someone wants to date so badly that they settle for dating anyone who's willing to date them whether they have anything in common or not?

- What are your hopes for dating?

Main Idea: Anyone can date. You just might not have met the right person yet. Keep looking and try to be patient!

Masturbation

Dear Jerome,

I'm 15 years old, and I am wondering about masturbation. To tell the truth, I sometimes do it in my room at night, but I heard somebody say I could go blind if I do it too often. Is that right?

Jake

Dear Jake,

First of all, masturbation is very normal and most people, both male and female, masturbate, at least at some point in their lives.

While masturbation is not usually talked about in public, and some people's values and religious beliefs may conflict with it, there is nothing about it that is harmful to a person. It is not dirty, evil, or harmful. It won't make you go blind, stunt your growth, turn you into a pervert, give you a sexually transmitted disease, make you sterile, or get you pregnant.

The most important thing to know about masturbation is that it is a very private thing that should always be done in private with the door closed. When masturbation is done in public, or in front of someone who does not wish to see it, it may be considered to be a crime. When done in a private place, however, within reasonable frequency, masturbation is perfectly normal.

Best wishes,

Jerome

 # Discussion Questions

- Why should masturbation always be done in private?

- When does masturbation become a "problem?"

- Why do you think there are so many myths about masturbation? (Example of a myth: If you masturbate, you will become blind.)

- Why don't you hear many people talk about masturbation?

Main Idea: Masturbation should be done in private, behind closed doors.

Are There Things You Just Don't Say?

Dear Jerome,

I am told that there are certain things that you don't say to a girl. I have no idea what that means. Could you fill me in on at least one?

Neil

Dear Neil,

Well, there are lots of things that could be taken the wrong way when dating a girl, and many of them have to do with what you think of how she looks. For now, I'll just point out one glaring example: The whole history of dating suggests that when a girl says, "Do these pants make my butt look big?" she really is looking for you to say that she is not fat, and that she is attractive. She is most likely looking for you to be polite instead of just being honest.

Many guys have walked into that trap and have said the "wrong" thing. For example, if you responded to her by saying something honest like: "You could really lose a few pounds," or "Yeah, your butt does look pretty huge in those jeans," she will most likely react by getting upset with you. Even though it may not seem like it since she's asking about her butt size, a good answer to give her in this situation is, "No. You look just fine." If you really don't feel comfortable saying this, you could say something like, "All that really matters is what you think. I'm happy with you the way you are."

Best wishes!

Jerome

Discussion Questions

- Why might a girl get upset with a guy for giving an honest answer to a question she asks about her appearance?

- Besides her weight, what else might a girl be overly concerned about?

- What are some nice compliments you could give another person in general?

- Is it better sometimes to be polite than it is to be very honest?

Main Idea: When a girl asks for a comment on her weight or appearance, she is usually looking for a reassuring statement such as: "You look just fine."

What Are They Talking About?

Dear Haley,

I'm thinking about asking this one girl out, but every time I see her out with her friends, there's always some word that comes up that I don't understand. It sounds to me like people are speaking words from another language. Is there any way I can figure this out?

Ben

Dear Ben,

Some words in our language are changing all the time, and it seems like teenagers are the ones who often introduce new words, mainly in the form of what is called slang. Slang simply means alternative ways of saying something. Examples of slang are the words "dude" meaning a guy, and the word "tight" meaning something interesting or cool.

The good news is that some slang words are used often and are used for an extended period of time. That being said, it may be worth your while to buy a book on slang words. You could also try writing unfamiliar slang words in a small notepad, and then ask someone you trust what those words mean.

Best wishes!

Haley

Discussion Questions

- What are some popular slang words that you hear?

- Why do you think slang words are invented?

- Can using slang words make you feel like you are a part of a group?

- What do you do if you don't understand what someone is talking about?

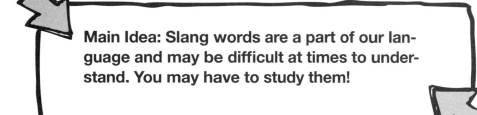

Main Idea: Slang words are a part of our language and may be difficult at times to understand. You may have to study them!

Resources

The following are resources that I found to be useful when considering the teenage years and Asperger Syndrome. This is by no means a comprehensive list, however. For more information about Asperger Syndrome and teen issues, check out your local library.

Attwood, T. (1998). *Asperger's Syndrome: A guide for parents and professionals.* London: Athenaeum Press.
This is one of the best books available on the topic of Asperger Syndrome (AS). It provides an excellent overview of what AS is and is considered to be "must have" as an AS resource.

Baron-Cohen, S. (2007). *Mind reading: The interactive guide to emotions*. London: Kingsley Publishers.
This helpful DVD includes six performers acting out 400+ emotions. It is a useful tool for anyone wishing to study human emotions.

Grandin, T., & Barron, S. (2005). *The unwritten rules of social relationships: Decoding social mysteries through the unique perspectives of autism.* Arlington, TX: Future Horizons, Inc.
Though not specific to either teenagers or dating, this book offers many valuable insights into socially correct behavior in general. It is especially powerful because it is written from the perspective of two people who have autism and have overcome some of their own social challenges. The section entitled "The Ten Unwritten Rules of Social Relationships" is particularly useful to someone with AS.

Jackson, L. (2002). *Freaks, geeks and Asperger Syndrome: A user guide to adolescence*. London: Jessica Kingsley Publishers.
Written by a 13-year-old with AS, this book offers a lot of practical advice both for teens with AS and adults who work with them. Examples of what to expect in the book include such topics as: School, fixations, sensory issues, bullying, and dating.

Mahler, K. J. (2009). *Hygiene and related behaviors for children and adolescents with autism spectrum and related disorders*. Shawnee Mission, KS: Autism Asperger Publishing Company.
Ranging from basic daily hygiene to picking, using public restrooms, burping, and farting, the topics in this curriculum focus on healthy and socially acceptable behaviors. Many of these impinge on the area of dating.

Myles, B. S., & Adreon, D. (2001). *Asperger Syndrome and adolescence: Practical solutions for school success*. Shawnee Mission, KS: Autism Asperger Publishing Company.
In this comprehensive and thorough book, the authors start with an overview of those characteristics of AS that make adolescence particularly challenging and difficult. The centerpiece of the book is a detailed discussion of strategies and supports necessary to ensure a successful school experience for students with AS at the middle and secondary levels – the very time when dating becomes an area of interest.

Myles, B. S., Trautman, M. L., & Schelvan, R. L. (2004). *The hidden curriculum: Practical solutions for understanding unstated rules in social situations.* Shawnee Mission, KS: Autism Asperger Publishing Company.
We are surrounded on a daily basis by unstated rules

and customs that make the world a confusing place for people on the autism spectrum. This applies to a great extent to the dating scene. Although not focusing specifically on dating, this book offers practical suggestions and advice for how a teacher, parent, or other professional can teach these social cues to the AS individual, and how the AS individual can understand these norms with help or individually.

Packer, A. J. (2004). *The how rude handbook of friendship and dating manners for teens: Surviving the social scene.* Minneapolis, MN: Free Spirit Publishing Inc. This book provides a good overview of how having good manners can help make the dating process go more smoothly. The question-and-answer section on dating may be particularly useful to someone with AS because it includes specific actions and things to say in a variety of dating situations.

Rabens, S. (2001). *The complete idiot's guide to dating for teens.* Indianapolis: Alpha Books. This book shares a detailed account of dating for teenagers. Though not written specifically for teens with AS, this book may be useful in that it explains many dating situations in detail. Particularly useful are "The Least You Need to Know" dating/relationship tips at the end of each section.

Santomauro, J., & Santomauro, D. (2007). *Asperger download: A guide to help teenage males with Asperger Syndrome trouble-shoot life's challenges.* Shawnee Mission, KS: Autism Asperger Publishing Company. While not exclusively targeting dating, this question-and-answer book written by a teenager with AS with comments by his mother contains many dating-related items. An easy read, it speaks directly to teenagers.

Stuart-Hamilton, I. (2004). *An Asperger dictionary of everyday expressions*. London: Jessica Kingsley Publishers, Ltd.
   This book provides an explanation of over 5,000 idiomatic expressions and is of particular interest to a person with AS because of its easy-to-use format and inclusion of a politeness level guide for the expressions.

Walsh, D. (2005). *Why do they act that way? A survival guide to the adolescent brain for you and your teen*. New York: Free Press.
   Though not specific to AS, this book offers many insights into the teenage world for parents of teens. In an easy-to-read-format, it explains what is going on in the teenage brain – both male and female – as well as strategies for how to deal with "teenage moments."

Useful Websites:

www.about.com
This is a good site in general for both teens and parents to explore issues in dating. Simply type "teens" into the search box to find lots of good information relevant to teens today.

www.autismsociety.org
This site provides useful information about autism in general, as well as a section specifically dedicated to teen issues.

www.webMD.com
A good website for a variety of topics including: Asperger definitions, teen slang, teens and dating, etc.